AQA PSYCHOLOGY AS YEAR 1 EXAMINATIONS. FOUR A* FULL MARK WHOLE PAPER EXAMPLES OF PAPER 1 (2 SETS) AND PAPER 2 (2 SETS).

By Joseph Anthony Campbell

First Printing: November 2020.

AQA PSYCHOLOGY AS YEAR 1 EXAMINATIONS. FOUR A* FULL MARK WHOLE PAPER EXAMPLES OF PAPER 1 (2 SETS) AND PAPER 2 (2 SETS).

CONTENTS

AUTHOR'S NOTE.

This book will provide you with crystal clear and accurate examples of 'A' star grade AQA AS level Psychology paper examinations from the current syllabus and enables students to achieve the same grade in their upcoming examinations.

I teach both GCSEs and A levels and I am a qualified and experienced teacher and tutor of over 17 years standing. I teach, write and provide independent tuition in Central and West London.

The resources in this book WILL help you get an A or A star in your AQA AS level Psychology examinations, as they have done and will continue to do so, for my students.

Best wishes,

Joseph

ABOUT THE AUTHOR.

I graduated from the Universities of Liverpool and Leeds and I obtained first class honours in my teacher training.

I have taught and provided private tuition for over 17 years up to University level. I also write academic resources for the Times Educational Supplement.

My tuition students have been fortunate enough to attain places to study at Oxford, Cambridge and Imperial College, London and other Russell Group Universities. The students have done very well in their examinations and one Psychology student even obtained full UMS marks in her A2 Psychology examination. I hope and know that my Psychology books can enable you to take the next step on your academic journey.

SUMMARY OF PSYCHOLOGY EXAMINATION PAPERS.

The examinations are linear i.e. they are all done at the end of each year.

There are **3** examination papers for Psychology A level.

(I have written further books to help you with the A level and I have provided details of the A level Psychology papers in those A level books).

There are **2** examination papers for Psychology AS level.

In this book, we are concerned with the 2 AS examinations which are completed at the end of Year 1 of your 'A' levels.

Paper **1** is divided into **3** sections:

Section A – Social Influence

Section B – Memory

Section C – Attachment

Each section is worth 24 marks and the paper has a total of 72 marks. There is 90 minutes for the exam (unless you have extra time).

Paper **2** is divided into **3** sections:

Section A – Approaches in Psychology

Section B – Psychopathology

Section C – Research Methods

Each section is worth 24 marks and the paper has a total of 72 marks. There is 90 minutes for the exam (unless you have extra time).

The exam structure is complicated. In each section there will be multiple choice questions, short answer questions and at least one extended writing question. This is why the examples in this book are particularly useful as you will need to familiarise yourself with these types of questions and their structure for each examination. They range from 1 to 12 marks per question.

ASSESSMENT OBJECTIVES.

There are three assessment objectives assessed in each examination: **AO1, AO2** and **AO3.**

AO1 = Outline. This involves outlining your knowledge and understanding. It involves recalling and describing theories, studies and methods.

AO2 = Apply. This involves applying your knowledge and understanding. You must apply your knowledge to different situations and contexts. You will apply this from the information given in the text provided in the question; which will be a theoretical or practical example.

AO3 = Evaluate. This involves analysing and interpreting. Evaluating studies and theories or drawing conclusions.

There may be one, two or all (only in the extended writing questions) of the assessment objectives in each question. Therefore, it is vitally important to be aware of the structure of how the assessment objectives are allocated in each question of the exam in order to maximise your opportunities to obtain full marks in each question.

It is worth noting that **the Assessment Objectives that are to be met for each question are not provided in the examination itself**, which provides a further complication for you. However, I have provided which assessment objectives are being assessed in the practice questions in this book to give you more awareness of what each type of question is looking for in the answer.

<u>Additional points to remember.</u>

1) **10% of your examination will be composed of mathematical questions**. But please do not be overly concerned, it is only GCSE level Mathematics and involves basic arithmetic, data and graphs.

2) **Approximately a third of all questions at AS and A level Psychology will involve Research Methods** and they can occur in any paper or section of your examination, not just in the Research Methods section. **Please make sure you apply a strong focus to Research Methods in your revision** and remember again that the Mathematics involved is only set at a GCSE level of difficulty.

3) When you are answering the A02 application section of the question, write 'In terms of application' before providing your AO2 points and give a quotation if possible, particularly if the question is asking you to 'refer' back to the information provided. Also, when you are answering the A03 evaluation section of the question, write 'In terms of evaluation' before providing your AO3 points.

4) Generally, my students prefer to separate the AO's out in their answers i.e. for a 12 mark (AO1 = 6; A03 =6) answer they will write 2

paragraphs with the first paragraph being AO1 (6 marks) and then the second paragraph being AO3 (6 marks) or 4 paragraphs with 3 marks of AO1 or A03 in each paragraph.

TIMINGS.

Please allocate minutes per mark! In Psychology AQA AS examinations Papers 1 and 2 there are 72 marks to aim for in 90 minutes, which works out at **1.25 minutes per mark**. (This is the same minutes per mark as in your 3 A level Papers also). Therefore, **if a question is worth 8 marks then you would spend roughly 10 minutes** on this question. In the examples in this book I have given you the maximum amount of time allowed for each question which always works out at **1.25 minutes per mark.**

A good rule of thumb is to apply the principle that you get **1 mark per correct point made in your answer** i.e. 4 good points for a 4-mark question. My students find that 1 mark per sentence also helps them to apply this rule generally. Similar to all the principles in this book, **you must apply and follow the correct timings for each question and stick to them throughout your exam to get an A or A star in your Psychology examinations.**

If you have extra time allocated to you, just change the calculation to accommodate the extra time you have for each mark i.e. approximately 1.5

minutes per mark if you have 25% extra time and 1.8 minutes per mark if you have 50% extra time. Allocate within your time management the time for checking if you wish but **move on from the set question as soon as you have reached or are coming towards your time limit**. This ensures that you have excellent coverage of your whole exam and therefore attain a very good mark.

Without applying this principle in these examinations (and to a large extent all examinations) you cannot achieve the highest marks! **Apply all of the principles provided in this book to succeed**!

APPROXIMATE WORD COUNT PER MARK IN PSYCHOLOGY.

Now that you know what is on each examination, how the assessment objectives are assessed and the time allocated for each type of question we come to what would be considered the correct word count per mark for each question. The primary principle though is to spend the right amount of time on each question as mentioned on the previous pages.

Unfortunately, there is no exact rule here as some questions are mathematical and do not require words whilst extended writing questions and essays tend to follow the set word count below more exactly.

In the answers in this book, I have provided the maximum word count for each answer which works out at **25 words per mark**. However, a good rule of thumb is between **15 and 25 words**.

15 words per mark – minimum word count.

20 words per mark – a generally good word count per mark.

25 words per mark – **The maximum word count generally in the time allocated.**

<u>Additional points to remember.</u>

1) If your answer has quality, 25 words per mark gives you the best chance of obtaining the highest marks in your Psychology exam. Obviously, it does not if you are waffling however. (Please remember to answer the question set and move on in the time allocated.)

2) Generally, Research Methods questions tend to need less words per mark but there are exceptions to this rule.

3) Remember: **Apply the principle that you get 1 mark per correct point made in your answer and 1 mark per sentence also helps to apply this rule** and if you are concise you can obtain each mark in 15 words of writing. I am aware that some students can write faster than others but all should be able to write 15 words per mark at A level in 1.25 minutes (if they have not been allocated extra time). This is where conciseness is important. However, using the principle of one point per sentence: **Each point/sentence and therefore mark should generally be between 15 and 25 words and completed in 1.25 minutes.**

4) My students have applied all the techniques I am providing you with to gain As and A stars in their Psychology examinations. You can replicate them by following the advice in this book.

AQA PSYCHOLOGY AS YEAR 1 EXAMINATIONS. FOUR A* FULL MARK WHOLE PAPER EXAMPLES OF PAPER 1 (2 SETS) AND PAPER 2 (2 SETS).

Very best wishes in your examinations! Joseph

SIX FURTHER STEPS TO EXAMINATION SUCCESS!

To gain confidence, we must work hard to gain a strong sense of self confidence. In order to ensure we are able to do this; following the 6 points below is key. These 6 points have been worked out through the process of preparing thousands of students for examination success.

1. Revise your subjects consistently and look up all of the words you do not understand in a dictionary, on a Kindle or through online search engines. This will ensure that you use the appropriate specialist vocabulary required by your subject in your examination.

2. Quality over quantity. Only write that which is very good. Never make a point you are not sure of and always come across as confident to the examiner.

3. Relax and believe; this breeds confidence.

4. Answer the question that is set. Do not answer the question you wish was on the examination and please do not waffle. Write your points and move on. Short sentences are often better and use paragraphs. If you are not sure what you are writing, please stop! Honesty is confidence;

waffling is dishonest writing. Your writing is part of who you are; please make sure that it reflects who you are accurately and fully. That it is of the highest standard.

5. Now that you know what is on each examination, how the assessment objectives are assessed, the time allocated for each type of question and what would be considered the correct word count per mark for each question; remember the primary principle: *To spend the right amount of time on each question* (needs to be mentioned twice).

6. Relax and believe (also needs to be mentioned twice). If you do the above, you will believe in yourself. You will not be nervous; you will believe and you will do well. No one is expecting you to write the most words ever written or to create a new way of thinking, please just write what you know and write it well in the time allocated and you will do very well. This also takes the pressure off you.

Always work hard; giving your best in a relaxed way. This leads to focus and, "Tachypsychia"– which is a speeding up of the mind which makes time appear to slow down and gives ease, comfort and quality to whatever it is that you are doing (in this case a Psychology exam).

AQA AS PSYCHOLOGY (7181/1) PAPER 1 INTRODUCTORY TOPICS IN PSYCHOLOGY. SPECIMEN MATERIAL (FIRST SET)

Section A
Social influence

Answer __all__ questions in this section (30 minutes for each section on Paper 1)

0 1 Briefly outline and evaluate the authoritarian personality as an explanation of obedience to authority.

[4 marks] (5 minutes) (AO1 = 2; AO3 = 2) (100 words maximum)

An authoritarian personality is a collection of traits developed from overly strict parenting. An authoritarian personality is more likely to be conformist and obey people of perceived higher status. (AO1 = 2)

It is difficult to establish cause and effect between overly strict parenting and later levels of obedience. It is also difficult to easily account for obedience of entire social groups/societies. (A03 = 2)

(59 Words total)

0 2 Read the item and then answer the question that follows.

The following article appeared in a newspaper:
Britain's views on homosexuality – the biggest social change of the last 30 years?
In the UK, views on homosexuality have changed significantly in recent times. Thirty years ago, almost two-thirds of the British public opposed same-sex relationships because they were 'morally wrong'. These days, homosexuality is accepted and the majority of British people support recent changes to the laws on gay marriage and adoption.
With reference to the article above, explain how social influence leads to social change.

[6 marks] (7.5 minutes) (AO2 = 6) (150 words maximum)

Factors affecting minority influence include consistency, commitment and flexibility. Social change occurs as viewed in the article above when the minority view, e.g. gay rights campaigners, challenges the majority view and is eventually accepted as the majority. This relates to conformity through the processes of informational social influence and internalisation. As the majority becomes more aware of the minority, they strive to understand the minority view and may internalise their views. The influence of obedience is also shown which leads to a social norm being created i.e. '...the majority of British people support recent changes to the laws on gay marriage and adoption.' Social cryptomnesia may also occur where people forget that the majority that is occurring now was once the minority.

(122 Words total)

0 3 Describe and evaluate two studies of social influence.

(12 marks) (15 minutes) (AO1 = 6; AO3 = 6) (300 words maximum)

Milgram's study used 40 male participants. They were assigned the role of 'teacher' and were shown a confederate being strapped to a pseudo-electric machine. The naive participants (NP's) had switches they were to press ranging from 15 volts to 450 volts. They were to shock the participants each time the confederate gave a wrong answer, increasing the voltage each time. The confederate gave the wrong answer each time. (AO1 = 3)

Evaluatively, the results showed that 100% of the participants went to 300 volts and 65% shocked the confederate with a 450-volt shock. This showed that when a legitimate authority figure (the psychologist in the white coat) orders a person to perform even a harmful action, they will often obey. However, the experiment lacks ecological validity as people are not normally asked to shock people. Also, the experiment is arguably ethically unsound as it caused the participants emotional distress and lacked informed consent.

(A03 = 3)

Zimbardo's study aimed to find out how much people conformed to roles. He used male student participants (an androcentric study like Milgram's) and randomly assigned the roles of prisoner or guard. The prisoners were mock arrested, stripped and numbered. The prisoners and guards formed groups and the prisoners became submissive and obedient to the guards. The experiment was abandoned after 6 days.

(AO1 = 3)

Evaluatively, Zimbardo aimed to show how ordinary people conform readily to roles. However, this experiment took place in an artificial environment and therefore lacks ecological validity. Zimbardo also acted as the prison superintendent in this experiment which could lead to observer bias and a clear conflict of interests. He, too, also caused his participants emotional distress as his participants appeared unaware at times of their right to withdraw.

(AO3 = 3)

(280 Words)

Section B
Memory

Answer <u>all</u> questions in this section (30 minutes for each section on Paper 1)

0 1 Read the item and then answer the questions that follow.

Participants in an experiment were shown a film of a robbery. The participants were then divided into two groups. One group was interviewed using a standard interview technique and the other group was interviewed using the cognitive interview technique. All participants were then given an 'accuracy score' (out of 20) based on how closely their recall matched the events in the film (20 = completely accurate, 0 = not at all accurate).

The results of the experiment are shown in Table 1.

Table 1: The median accuracy score for the standard interview and the cognitive interview.

	Standard interview	Cognitive interview
Median	10	15

The experiment used an independent groups design. Explain how this study could have been modified by using a matched pairs design.

[4 marks] (5 minutes) (AO3 = 4) (100 words maximum)

The researcher needs to ensure that the two groups are matched for key variables, such as eyesight, age and intelligence. These variables may affect memory in this situation. All participants should be tested beforehand as regards these variables. Finally, for each person in one condition, the researcher should assign a 'matched' person in the other condition.

(56 Words total)

0 2 Identify and outline two techniques that may be used in a cognitive interview.

[4 marks] (5 minutes) (AO1 = 4) (100 words maximum)

Changing perspective – the interviewee recalls from different perspectives e.g. how it would have appeared to other witnesses.
Report everything – the interviewer encourages the interviewee to recall and report everything they remember, even though it may seem irrelevant.

(37 words total)

0 3 Outline and evaluate research into the effects of leading questions on the accuracy of eyewitness testimony.

[8 marks] (10 minutes) (AO1 = 4; AO3 = 4) (200 words maximum)

Loftus and Palmer conducted studies into eyewitness testimony in 1974. They played a video of a car crash to participants and asked them 'how fast was the car going when it...the other car'. In different conditions they found that if they used the word 'smashed' the participants estimated an average speed of 41 miles per hour compared to an average estimation of 32 miles per hour if they used the word 'contacted'. A week later they also asked 'Did you see any broken glass?' using the word 'smashed' for one group, 'hit' for another and a third control group had no indication of speed given to them. The 'smashed' group had a higher number reporting 'broken glass', even though there was none.
(AO1=4)
In evaluating, we are aware that viewing a car crash on video is not as emotionally stimulating and produces less adrenaline than being in a real car crash and this may affect the results as it is also less ecologically valid. The participants may have also guessed the aims of the experiment and thus shown demand characteristics. However,

both experiments also show that leading questions may have a long-term effect on eyewitness testimony. (A03=4) **(195 words total)**

Section C

Attachment

*Answer **all** questions in this section (30 minutes for each section on Paper 1)*

0 1 Read the item and then answer the question that follows.

Proud father Abdul was talking to his friend, as they were both watching Abdul's wife, Tasneem, interacting with their baby daughter, Aisha.
'It's amazing really', said Abdul. 'Tasneem smiles, Aisha smiles back. Tasneem moves her head,
Aisha moves hers, perfectly in time with each other.'
'Yes', agreed the friend. 'It's almost as if they are one person.'

With reference to Abdul's conversation with his friend, outline two features of caregiver-infant interaction.

[4 marks] (5 minutes) (AO2 = 4) (100 words maximum)

Imitation – infant copies/mimics adult. This is shown when, 'Tasneem smiles, Aisha smiles back.'

Interactional synchrony – infant and adult react and respond in time to sustain communication. This is shown when the friend says, 'It's almost as if they are one person'.

(41 words)

0 2 Read the item and then answer the question that follows.

Studies of attachment often involve observation of interactions between mother and baby pairs like Tasneem and Aisha. Researchers sometimes write down everything that happens as it takes place, including their own interpretation of the events.

Explain how such observational research might be refined through the use of behavioural categories.

[4 marks] (5 minutes) (AO3 = 4) (100 words maximum)

Clear focus – using categories provides clear focus for the researcher. Categories also enable the proposal of a testable hypothesis. Behavioural categories also allow observers to tally observations into pre-arranged groupings and to allow for more objective/scientific data recording.

(38 words)

0 3 Read the item and then answer the question that follows.

Joe was taken away from his alcoholic parents at six months old and placed in care. He was adopted when he was seven years old, but has a difficult relationship with his adoptive parents. He is aggressive towards his younger siblings and is often in trouble at school. His last school report said, 'Joe struggles with classwork and seems to have little regard for the feelings of others.'

Discuss Bowlby's maternal deprivation theory. Refer to the experience of Joe as part of your discussion.

[12 marks] (15 minutes) (AO1 = 6; AO2 = 2; AO3= 4) (300 words maximum)

Bowlby's maternal deprivation theory could explain why Joe 'has a difficult relationship with his adoptive parents.' This could be because Joe may have formed a single monotropic attachment to his mother until he was 'six months old' which would have been broken when he was 'placed in care'. Bowlby believed in a critical period for forming attachments and as Joe was adopted at 'seven years old' Joe is beyond the critical period for forming attachments. According to Bowlby if attachment is disrupted or not formed during the critical period then an attachment will not be formed.

Joe also appears unable to form secure social bonds, which explains why he is 'aggressive towards his younger siblings.' Bowlby also stated that a consequence of maternal deprivation was a low IQ (Intelligence Quota) which may explain why Joe 'struggles with classwork'. As his critical period was spent in care, Joe's difficult relationships may be due to a lack of opportunity to develop an internal working model. Bowlby stated that the internal working model acted as a template for later relationships. This may mean that Joe is both intellectually and emotionally stunted.

Joe's absence of a monotropic bond and therefore his maternal deprivation could also link to delinquency, according to Bowlby. This is potentially demonstrated as he is 'often in trouble at school' and may have affectionless psychopathy according to Bowlby as he has 'little regard for the feelings of others'. However, some believe that Bowlby overemphasised the role of the mother and monotropy upon a child's development and further to the contrasting views of other psychologists it was Bowlby himself who stated in later years that a monotropic bond could also form securely with the father.

(283 words)

AQA AS PSYCHOLOGY (7181/1) PAPER 1 INTRODUCTORY TOPICS IN PSYCHOLOGY. SPECIMEN MATERIAL (SECOND SET)

Section A
Social influence

Answer <u>all</u> questions in this section (30 minutes for each section on Paper 1)

0 1 Many people have criticised Zimbardo's prison study.
Identify and briefly discuss two reasons why people have criticised Zimbardo's prison study.

[6 marks] (7.5 minutes) (AO1 = 2; AO3 = 4) (150 words maximum)

Two reasons that people have criticised Zimbardo's prison study are for the reasons that they believed it to be unethical as firstly it led to psychological harm as the participants soon became distressed and secondly for the fact that Zimbardo himself took part in the experiment and was a participant observer.
(AO1=2)
The distress of the participants should have been anticipated beforehand and informed consent should have been gained before the experiment began. Zimbardo caused the participants to have emotional distress and the participants appeared unaware at times of their right to withdraw. Zimbardo also acted as the prison superintendent in this experiment which could lead to observer bias and demonstrates a clear conflict of interests. Thus, the overall validity of the findings themselves could be questioned.
(AO3=4)

(126 words)

0 2 Social influence research helps us to understand how it is possible to change people's behaviour: for example, understanding how to persuade people to eat more healthily.
With reference to this example of social change, explain how psychology might affect the economy.

[4 marks] (5 minutes) (AO2 = 4) (100 words maximum)

Social influence research informs us how both behaviour and attitudes can be changed. For example, how minority influence can be exerted or how people tend to conform to perceived norms. In the example listed above, the resulting change of eating more healthily leads to an increase in the general health of these people. This has an economic implication and saves health services and care resources and potentially increases economic production through less people taking time off work.

(77 words)

0 3 Read the item and then answer the question that follows.

Polly always checks what her friends are going to wear before she gets ready to go out because she does not like to be the odd one out. Jed watches his colleagues carefully when he starts a new job so that he can work out where to put his things and how long to take for lunch.

Discuss two explanations for conformity. Refer to Polly and Jed in your discussion.

[12 marks] (15 minutes) (AO1 = 6; AO2 = 2; AO3 = 4) (300 words maximum)

Normative social influence occurs when people conform in order to be a part of the majority and to not stand out. Normative social influence often, but not always, results in compliance or a superficial change in behaviour. Informational social influence occurs when people conform in order to be fully aware as to how to behave in a given situation and therefore use the majority as a source of information. This often results in internalisation i.e. adopting the views and behaviours of the majority. (AO1=4)

Polly's behaviour is due to normative social influence because she desires to be the same as everyone else and to be a part of the 'norm'. Jed is using his colleagues as a

source of information which is informational social influence. He will learn 'where to put his things' and take the appropriate amount of time for lunch.
(A01=2; A02 = 2)

Informational social influence tends to have a more permanent effect whereas normative social influence tends to be more transient. There is also the possibility of an overlap between the two types of social influence as we often look to others for information but partly because we do not want to be different.
(A03=2)

In Asch's (1951) study upon conformity as regards an unambiguous task, 37% were wrong and conformed to the majority due to normative social influence. However different conditions of the study illustrated both normative and informational social influence supporting the idea of an overlap between these two explanations of conformity.
(A03=2)

(242 words)

Section B
Memory

Answer __all__ questions in this section (30 minutes for each section on Paper 1)

0 1 Read the item and then answer the questions that follow.

A researcher investigating the multi-store model of memory tested short-term memory by reading out loud sequences of numbers that participants then had to repeat aloud immediately after presentation. The first sequence was made up of three numbers: for example, 8, 5, 2. Each participant was tested several times, and each time the length of the sequence was increased by adding another number.

Use your knowledge of the multi-store model of memory to explain the purpose of this research and the likely outcome.

[4 marks] (5 minutes) (AO2 = 4) (100 words maximum)

The purpose of this research is to test the capacity of short-term memory. Short-term memories are coded both verbally and acoustically and this research requires verbal rehearsal. The outcome would most likely be that most of the people tested would be able to repeat correctly a sequence of between 5 and 9 items. This is because according to the multi-store model, short-term memory has a limited capacity of between 5 and 9 items.

(73 words)

0 2 After the study was completed, the researcher decided to modify the study by using sequences of letters rather than numbers.

Suggest one 4-letter sequence and one 5-letter sequence that the researcher could use. In the case of each sequence, give a justification for your choice. Use a different justification for each sequence.

[4 marks] (5 minutes) (AO2 = 4) (100 words maximum)

ZXLM is the appropriate 4-letter sequence I would suggest. This is because it has no recognisable abbreviations which have meaning and can be recalled as a whole.

JXFKD is the appropriate 5-letter sequence I would suggest. This is because it has no rhyming letters, which would mean that the cognitive demand would be reduced for the participants and could influence the research (if it contained rhyming letters).

(67 words)

0 3 Read the item and then answer the question that follows.

Martin is studying for his modern language exams. He revises French followed by Spanish on the same night and then gets confused between the two: for example, he remembers the French word for 'chair' instead of the Spanish word for 'chair'. Sometimes, his mum helps to test Martin's vocabulary. When he is unable to remember a word, his mum tells him the first letter, then he can often recall it correctly.

Discuss two explanations for forgetting. Refer to Martin's experiences in your answer.

[12 marks] (15 minutes) (AO1 = 6; AO2 = 2; AO3 = 4) (300 words maximum)

Interference is an explanation for forgetting as two sets of information can become confused, such as Spanish and French in Martin's case when he gets confused between the two. There are two types of interference; proactive interference and retroactive interference. Proactive interference is when old learning prevents the recall of more recent information, shown when Martin 'remembers the French word for 'chair' instead of the Spanish word for 'chair'' as Martin 'revises French followed by Spanish'.

Retroactive interference is when new learning prevents the recall of previously learned information. As French and Spanish are similar types of material this makes interference more likely. There is a question as to whether interference involves the over-writing of other information and it is said that semantic memory is more resistant to interference than other types of memory.

Retrieval failure which is also known as cue-dependent forgetting has also been posited as an explanation for forgetting. This is demonstrated when information is available but cannot be recalled because of the absence of appropriate cues. The types of cues that have been studied by psychologists include context, state and organisation. Cues improve recall if recall takes place in the same context as learning, if the person is in the same physical state as when the material was learned and if triggers or categories are assigned in order to achieve cue-dependent learning. For example, Martin's mum gives him cues, 'tells him the first letter' which can then be used for him to access the material he has failed to retrieve.

Both explanations for forgetting have general implications for both revision and other situations.

(267 words)

Section C
Attachment

*Answer **all** questions in this section (30 minutes for each section on Paper 1)*

0 1 Read the item and then answer the questions that follow.

A child psychologist carried out an overt observation of caregiver-infant interaction. She observed a baby boy interacting separately with each of his parents. Using a time sampling technique, she observed the baby with each parent for 10 minutes. Her findings are shown in Table 1 below.

Table 1: Frequency of each behaviour displayed by the infant when interacting with his mother and when interacting with his father

	Gazing at parent	Looking away from parent	Eyes closed	Total
Mother	12	2	6	20
Father	6	10	4	20
Total	18	12	10	40

Using the data in Table 1, explain the procedure used for the time sampling technique in this study.

[3 marks] (3.75 minutes) (AO2 = 3) (75 words maximum)

The total observation time for each parent was 10 minutes. The psychologist made 20 observations for each parent. To generate 20 observations for each parent she must therefore have recorded her observation every 30 seconds.

(35 words)

0 2 In what percentage of the total observations was the baby gazing at his mother? Show your calculations.
[2 marks] (2.5 minutes) (AO2 = 2)

12 / 40 = 0.3
0.3 x 100 = 30%
Answer = 30%

0 3 The study in Question 09 was an overt observation.
Explain what is meant by 'overt observation'.

[2 marks] (2.5 minutes) (AO1 = 2) (50 words maximum)

Overt observation is when the observer is clearly visible and not hidden from view. Also, the people who are being observed know that they are being observed.

(27 words)

0 4 Outline the procedure used in one study of animal attachment.

[4 marks] (5 minutes) (AO1 = 4) (100 words maximum)

Harlow aimed to find out whether baby rhesus monkeys would prefer a source of food or a source of comfort and protection as an attachment figure. In laboratory experiments the rhesus monkeys were raised in isolation. They had two 'surrogate' mothers. One was made of wire mesh and contained a feeding bottle; the other was made of cloth but did not contain a feeding bottle.

(65 words)

0 5 Briefly discuss one limitation of using animals to study attachment in humans.

[4 marks] (5 minutes) (AO3 = 4) (100 words maximum)

There are problems of anthropomorphic extrapolation in applying the results to human infants. What applies to non-human species may not also apply to human infants. For example, Lorenz studied imprinting in geese, which are a precocial species i.e. they have their eyes open and walk from birth. This is very different to humans who cannot walk for a few years. Therefore, attachment studies using animals should be studied carefully.

(69 words)

0 6 One theory about how and why babies form attachments is Bowlby's monotropic theory.

Outline and evaluate Bowlby's monotropic theory of attachment

[8 marks] (10 minutes) (AO1 = 4; AO3 = 4) (200 words maximum)

According to Bowlby we have evolved a biological need to attach to our main caregiver. His idea is called monotropy and it states that we form one main attachment, usually to our biological mother. This attachment has survival value as staying close to our mother ensures food and protection. It also gives us a 'template' for all future relationships as we learn to trust and care for others. This forms an internal working model for all later attachments. The first three years of life are posited by Bowlby as the 'critical period' for attachment to develop or it may never do so.
(AO1=4)

In terms of evaluation, however, Schaffer et al provided evidence against Bowlby's theory. They found that many children form multiple attachments and may not attach to their mother. This contrasts with Bowlby's theory of monotropy. Also, in Harlow's study other monkeys who did not have a primary caregiver but grew up together, seemed to attach to each other instead and showed no signs of social or emotional disturbance in later life.

(A03=4)

(173 words)

AQA AS PSYCHOLOGY (7181/2) PAPER 2 PSYCHOLOGY IN CONTEXT. SPECIMEN MATERIAL (FIRST SET)

Section A
Approaches in Psychology

Answer __all__ questions in this section (30 minutes for each section on Paper 2)

0 1 Read the item and then answer the question that follows.

Psychologists investigating theoretical models of cognitive processing study human cognitive processing. They sometimes give participants problems to solve then ask them about the experience afterwards. Typical participant responses are as follows:
Response A: 'There were too many things to think about at the same time.'
Response B: 'I had to do one task at a time, then do the next task, and so on.'

Briefly suggest how each of these responses might inform psychologists investigating models of human cognitive processing.

[2 marks] (2.5 minutes) (AO2 = 2) (50 words maximum)

Response A shows that processing has limited capacity and response B demonstrates that in order for a participant to complete demanding or new processes they must do them sequentially.

(29 words)

0 2 Read the item and then answer the questions that follow.

A behaviourist researcher studying reinforcement carried out a laboratory experiment. He put a cat in a puzzle box. The cat was able to escape from the puzzle box by pulling on a string which opened the door. Each time the cat escaped it was given a food treat. At first, the cat escaped quite slowly, but with each attempt the escape time decreased.

Explain which type of conditioning is being investigated in this experiment?

[2 marks] (2.5 minutes) (AO2 = 2) (50 words maximum)

Operant conditioning is being investigated in this experiment as the cat is rewarded with food to positively reinforce certain behaviour, in this case 'pulling the string'.

(26 words)

0 3 Read the item and then answer the questions that follow.

A psychologist carried out a study of social learning. As part of the procedure, he showed children aged 4-5 years a film of a 4-year-old boy stroking a puppy. Whilst the children watched the film, the psychologist commented on how kind the boy was. After the children had watched the film, the psychologist brought a puppy into the room and watched to see how the children behaved with the puppy.

Outline what is meant by social learning theory and explain how social learning might have occurred in the procedure described above.

[6 marks] (7.5 minutes) (AO1 = 2; AO2 = 4) (150 words maximum)

Social learning theory (SLT) states that individuals can learn from role models. An individual may observe and imitate and therefore model themselves on another person i.e. modelling. This role model is usually someone that the person can identify with e.g. they are of a similar age or the same gender. Behaviour can also be taught through positive and negative reinforcement and vicarious reinforcement.
(AO1=2)

In this experiment SLT is taking place as the psychologist provided the children with a role model the same age as them acting pro-socially by 'stroking a puppy.' The children were also encouraged to identify with the role model and this makes them highly likely to imitate him. This acted as vicarious reinforcement and the children may imitate his behaviour in the hope of being praised although some may not perform these actions due to the internalisation of the model not being visibly manifested immediately.

(A02=4)

(148 words)

0 4 Discuss two limitations of social learning theory.

[6 marks] (7.5 minutes) (AO3 = 6) (150 words maximum)

Social learning theory posits that behaviours are learnt from the environment and this does not explain how some behaviours appear to be innate such as reflexes. Furthermore, SLT is unable to explain abstract notions such as justice or fairness. It explains the learning of outward behaviours but not abstract notions which are less simplistic and which cannot be observed directly.

Psychologists are also unable to establish cause and effect (causal relationship) when studying SLT. This is because SLT may not produce outward behaviours at the time that the original learning took place. It may be a significant period of time before these observed behaviours are internalised and thus manifested. Although Bandura's research-controlled variables and had replicable results it is still difficult to establish this cause and effect in real life.

(130 words)

Section B

Psychopathology

Answer all questions in this section (30 minutes for each section on Paper 2)

0 1 Read the item and then answer the questions that follow.

Researchers analysed the behaviour of over 4000 pairs of twins. The results showed that the degree to which obsessive-compulsive disorder (OCD) is inherited is between 45% and 65%.

Distinguish between obsessions and compulsions.

[2 marks] (2.5 minutes) (AO1 = 2) (50 words maximum)

Obsessions are intrusive and persistent thoughts that can lead someone to act upon their compulsions. These compulsions are actions such as obsessive hand washing that temporarily reduce the anxiety of the obsessive thoughts.

(33 words)

0 2 With reference to the study described above, what do the results seem to show about possible influences on the development of OCD?

[4 marks] (5 minutes) (AO2 = 4) (100 words maximum)

This study demonstrates that obsessive-compulsive disorder (OCD) may/does have a genetic basis. This is shown as between 45% to 65% of OCD is inherited, which supports a biological basis for the development of OCD.

However, there is still 35% to 55% of OCD that is not inherited, showing that there must be other components to the development of OCD such as cognitive and behavioural abnormalities.

(65 words)

0 3 Read the item and then answer the question that follows.

Steven describes how he feels when he is in a public place. 'I always have to look out for people who might be ill. If I come into contact with people who look ill, I think I might catch it and die. If someone starts to cough or sneeze then I have to get away and clean myself quickly.'

Outline one cognitive characteristic of OCD and one behavioural characteristic of OCD that can be identified from the description provided by Steven.

[2 marks] (2.5 minutes) (AO2 = 2) (50 words maximum)

A cognitive characteristic is that Steven has obsessive thoughts e.g. 'to look out for people who might be ill'. This is also known as hyper vigilance.
A behavioural characteristic is the compulsion that Steven has that he must 'get away and clean myself quickly' if someone sneezes or coughs.

(49 words)

0 4 Briefly outline one strength of the cognitive explanation of depression.

[2 marks] (2.5 minutes) (AO3 = 2) (50 words maximum)

The cognitive explanation of depression takes into account the thoughts and beliefs of an individual and this has led to a lessening of negative thoughts and beliefs in individuals through effective treatments for depression; which have been based on previous experimental research.

(42 words)

0 5 Outline and evaluate the behavioural approach to treating phobias.
[12 marks] (15 minutes) (AO1 = 6; AO3 = 6) (300 words maximum)

The behavioural approach to treating phobias consists of systematic desensitisation and flooding. Flooding consists of putting an individual into a place or a scenario or into a visualisation of their set phobia i.e. such as arachnophobia- the fear of spiders. This would trigger their phobia immediately and they would be left to face their phobia until their anxiety levels decline and their phobia is eliminated. This method is immediate and fairly inexpensive leading to more accessibility for people to eliminate their phobia. However, some argue that it is unethical as it causes the patient emotional distress. Also, if they leave before their phobia is fully extinguished it can heighten or worsen their phobic levels.

Systematic desensitisation involves gradually working up a patients fear hierarchy until the patient is able to maintain a relaxed state when confronted with the situation that triggers their phobia the most such as holding a spider if arachnophobic. As the patient moves upwards on the hierarchical scale, they may have their treatment initiated by simply viewing a picture of a spider. The patient is taught relaxation techniques beforehand such as deep breathing in order to apply these techniques as their anxiety is triggered whilst moving up the fear hierarchy. Systematic desensitisation uses
counter-conditioning which results in the patient no longer associating the stimulus with danger and thus anxiety.

Zinbarg et al (1992) found that systematic desensitisation was the most effective of all contemporary treatments and Ost et al found that 90% of patients experienced anxiety reduction after just one session in both flooding and systematic desensitisation. Behavioural therapy also treats symptoms rather than cognitive behavioural therapy which focuses more on the causes of anxiety.

(278 words)

Section C
Research Methods

Answer all questions in this section (30 minutes for each section on Paper 2)

0 1 Read the item and then answer the questions that follow.

A psychologist wanted to see if creativity is affected by the presence of other people. To test this, he arranged for 30 people to participate in a study that involved generating ideas for raising funds for a local youth club. Participants were randomly allocated to one of two conditions.

Condition A: there were 15 participants in this condition. Each participant was placed separately in a room and was given 40 minutes to think of as many ideas as possible for raising funds for a local youth club. The participant was told to write down his or her ideas and these were collected in by the psychologist at the end of the 40 minutes.

Condition B: there were 15 participants in this condition. The participants were randomly allocated to 5 groups of equal size. Each group was given 40 minutes to think of as many ideas as possible for raising funds for a local youth club. Each group was told to write down their ideas and these were collected by the psychologist at the end of the 40 minutes.

The psychologist counted the number of ideas generated by the participants in both conditions and calculated the total number of ideas for each condition.

Table 2: Total number of ideas generated in Condition A (when working alone) and in Condition B (when working in a group)

	Condition A Working alone	Condition B Working in a group
Total number of ideas generated	110	75

Identify the experimental design used in this study and outline one advantage of this experimental design.

[3 marks] (4.5 minutes) (AO1 = 1; AO3 = 2) (75 words maximum)

The experimental design used is an independent groups design; an advantage of this is that there are no order effects. This means that no participant improves with practice i.e. learning effect or has their performance negatively affected by fatigue effect.

(40 words)

0 2 Describe one other experimental design that researchers use in psychology.

[2 marks] (2.5 minutes) (AO1 = 2) (50 words maximum)

Another experimental design used is a repeated measures design. This is when all the participants participate in all the conditions.

(20 words)

0 3 Apart from using random allocation, suggest one way in which the psychologist might have improved this study by controlling for the effects of extraneous variables. Justify your answer.

[2 marks] (2.5 minutes) (AO3 = 2) (50 words maximum)

The psychologist could have tested all of the participants in the same room as this would ensure that participants will not receive cues from their surroundings and that extraneous variables will not interfere with the experiment's findings.

(37 words)

0 4 Write a suitable hypothesis for this study.

[3 marks] (3.75 minutes) (AO2 = 3) (75 words maximum)

Those participants that work on their own and those that work in groups are equally likely to generate ideas. (Null hypothesis and non-directional.)

(23 words)

0 5 From the information given in the description, calculate the number of participants in each group in Condition B.

[1 mark] (1.25 minutes) (AO2 = 1)

15/5 = 3

0 6 Read the item and then answer the questions that follow.

The psychologist noticed that the number of ideas generated by each of the individual participants in Condition A varied enormously whereas there was little variation in performance between the 5 groups in Condition B. He decided to calculate a measure of dispersion for each condition.

Name a measure of dispersion the psychologist could use.

[1 mark] (1.25 minutes) (AO1 = 1)

Standard deviation.

0 7 The psychologist uses the measure of dispersion you have named in your answer to question 0 6. State how the result for each condition would differ.

[1 mark] (1.25 minutes) (AO2 =1) (25 words maximum)

The standard deviation would be greater in condition A than in condition B.

(13 words)

0 8 Explain how the psychologist could have used random allocation to assign the 15 participants in Condition B into the 5 groups.

[3 marks] (3.75 minutes) (AO2 = 3) (75 words maximum)

The psychologist could have numbered the participants between 1 and 15. He could then put the 15 numbers in a hat. He could then draw out 3 numbers to create the first group and repeat the process until all participants are in five groups of 3.

(46 words)

0 9 Using the information given, explain how the psychologist could further analyse the data using percentages.

[2 marks] (2.5 minutes) (AO3 = 2) (50 words maximum)

The psychologist would add the total number of ideas generated in both conditions which is 185. The psychologist then divides each condition by 185 and multiplies this by 100 to receive the percentage.

(33 words)

1 0 At the end of the study the psychologist debriefed each participant. Write a debriefing that the psychologist could read out to the participants in Condition A.

[6 marks] (7.5 minutes) (AO2 =6) (150 words maximum)

The aim of this experiment is to discern whether working in groups affected the number of ideas generated in comparison to working alone. The study consisted of two conditions of which you would have been assigned to either condition A or condition B. Condition A consisted of one person generating ideas and condition B consisted of a group generating ideas.

You will be informed of the results at a later date and your data will be kept wholly anonymous. Your welfare is of vital importance and if you have any questions or ethical concerns please feel free to talk to the researcher. You retain the right to withdraw at this point and we wish to thank you for taking part in this experiment. We hope it has been a worthwhile experience for you.

(133 words)

AQA AS PSYCHOLOGY (7181/2) PAPER 2 PSYCHOLOGY IN CONTEXT. SPECIMEN MATERIAL (SECOND SET)

Section A

Approaches in Psychology

Answer <u>all</u> questions in this section (30 minutes for each section on Paper 2)

0 1 Briefly explain one function of the endocrine system.

[2 marks] (2.5 minutes) (AO1 = 2) (50 words maximum)

The endocrine system involves glands which secrete hormones. The adrenal gland produces the hormone adrenaline which is responsible for our 'fight or flight (or freeze – Cannon 1927)' reaction when we are stressed.

(33 words)

0 2 A cognitive psychologist investigating how memory works gave participants the same word list to recall in one of two conditions. All the words were of equal difficulty.

Condition 1: Ten participants recalled the words in the same room in which they had learned the words.

Condition 2: Ten different participants recalled the words in a room that was not the same room as that in which they had learned the words.

The following results were obtained:

Table 1: Mean values and standard deviations for Condition 1 and Condition 2 in a memory experiment.

	Condition 1	Condition 2
Mean	15.9	10.6
Standard deviation	3.78	1.04

Why are the standard deviation values found in the study above useful descriptive statistics for the cognitive psychologist?

[2 marks] (2.5 minutes) (AO2 = 2) (50 words maximum)

Standard deviation values show the amount of variation across a set of values or a spread of scores and the range and delineate participant variables (condition 1 indicates there were more variables than condition 2).

(35 words)

0 3 Outline one problem of studying internal mental processes like memory ability by conducting experiments such as that described in Question 03 above.

[2 marks] (2.5 minutes) (AO3 = 2) (50 words maximum)

In an internal mental process, the researcher is unable to observe the process. This provides a problem as the researcher has to infer what processes are taking place by the behaviour the participant exhibits and this can easily lead to errors.

(41 words)

0 4 Rita and Holly are identical twins who were separated at birth. When they finally met each other at the age of 35, they were surprised at how different their personalities were. Rita is much more social and outgoing than Holly.

Use your knowledge of genotype and phenotype to explain this difference in their personalities.

[4 marks] (5 minutes) (AO2 = 4) (100 words maximum)

As Rita and Holly are monozygotic twins their genotypes are the same. This means that genetically they carry the same genetic predispositions. However, it is possible that external factors may contribute to their development also such as differing environments and this could begin to explain why Rita and Holly have such different phenotypes. One possible explanation for their difference in phenotypes may be due to Rita formerly being placed in situations were being sociable was rewarded whilst Holly was not.

(80 words)

0 5 Outline and evaluate the social learning theory approach. Refer to evidence in your answer.

[12 marks] (15 minutes) (A01 = 6; AO3 = 6) (300 words maximum)

Social learning theory states that individuals can learn from role models. An individual may observe and imitate and therefore model themselves on another person. This is known as modelling. This role model must be someone that the person can identify with e.g. they are of a similar age or the same gender. Social leaning theory approach (SLT) states that behaviour can also be taught through positive and negative reinforcement and vicarious reinforcement (seeing others being rewarded for certain behaviours). For effective learning, meditational processes must also take place, such as attention which involves an attentional focus on the behaviour being copied and reproduction which involves judging whether you are able to imitate the behaviour observed.
(AO1 = 6)

In terms of evaluation, there is evidence to support SLT such as Bandura's study on the imitation of aggression. This study showed that children who were exposed to

aggressive models tend to imitate the aggressive model's behaviour. However, because the learning is internalised and the learning could take place long before the behaviour is exhibited, it is hard to establish cause and effect when studying SLT. SLT is also reductionist; reducing complex phenomena to simplistic terminology and fails to take into account any other explanations for learning such as biological or genetic influences. SLT also does not explain the cognitive processes that cause an individual to want to copy a role model or certain behaviours that they demonstrate. SLT does however explain human traits which the behavioural approach neglects.
(AO3 =6) **(244 words)**

Section B

Psychopathology

Answer all questions in this section (30 minutes for each section on Paper 2)

0 1 What is meant by 'statistical infrequency' as a definition of abnormality?

[2 marks] (2.5 minutes) (AO1 = 2) (50 words maximum)

This is when an individual's traits widely differ to that of the average population. It is when they fall either side of a bell curve of the population on a graph for example, if an individual's intelligence quota (IQ) was 150 and the average populations was 100.

(47 words)

0 2 Gavin describes his daily life.

'I sometimes get gripped with the thought that my family is in danger. In particular, I worry about them being trapped in a house fire. I now find that I can only calm myself if I check that every plug socket is switched off so an electrical fire couldn't start. I used to switch each socket on and off, but now I have to press each switch six times. It takes me ages to leave the house.'

Outline two characteristics of obsessive-compulsive disorder. Refer to Gavin in your answer.

[4 marks] (5 minutes) (AO1 = 2; AO2 = 2) (100 words maximum)

One characteristic is that Gavin has persistent and recurring thoughts which are characteristic of the obsessive component of obsessive-compulsive disorder (OCD). An example of this is shown when he states, 'I sometimes get gripped with the thought that my family is in danger'.

A second characteristic is that Gavin also has compulsions; shown through partaking in repetitive actions that temporarily reduce the anxiety caused by the obsessions. Gavin has to 'press each switch six times' in order to calm his obsessions. This is also characteristic of OCD.

(87 words)

0 3 Read the item and then answer the question that follows.

Tommy is six years old and has a phobia about birds. His mother is worried because he now refuses to go outside. She says, 'Tommy used to love playing in the garden and going to the park to play football with his friends, but he is spending more and more time watching TV and on the computer.'

A psychologist has suggested treating Tommy's fear of birds using systematic desensitisation.

Explain how this procedure could be used to help Tommy overcome his phobia.

[4 marks] (5 minutes) (AO2 = 4) (100 words maximum)

Tommy would be taught relaxation techniques, i.e. deep breathing. Tommy would then devise a fear hierarchy scale with the situation that triggers his phobia the most at the top of the hierarchical scale such as holding a bird and the situation that triggers his phobia the least at the bottom, such as looking at a picture of a bird. Tommy would then work his way up the hierarchical scale by being exposed to his phobia of birds gradually and then move up to the next item on the hierarchical scale when he is no longer anxious with a set stage.

(100 words)

0 4 Explain why systematic desensitisation might be more ethical than using flooding to treat Tommy's phobia.

[2 marks] (2.5 minutes) (AO3 = 2) (50 words maximum)

Flooding involves making a person confront their phobia fully until their anxiety has worn off. However, Tommy's anxiety levels may increase dramatically though flooding whilst systematic desensitisation is more gradual and limits the levels of anxiety experienced by the participant.

(40 words)

0 5 Outline and evaluate at least one cognitive approach to explaining depression.

[12 marks] (15 minutes) (AO1 = 6; AO3 = 6) (300 words maximum)

Ellis' ABC model posits that depression originates with an activating event such as the break-up of a relationship which then leads to an irrational belief such as 'I am unlovable'. This belief results in a consequence which may lead to depression.
(AO1=3)

Beck's negative triad posits that a person is depressed because they have negative thoughts about themselves (I am unlovable), the world (no one will ever love me because I am unlovable) and the future (this will continue forever).
(AO1=3)

The cognitive models above offer a useful approach to explaining depression as thoughts and feelings are taken into account. Cognitive behavioural therapies have also successfully treated depression. Psychologists have also demonstrated that depressed participants have more negative thoughts than non-depressed participants and this demonstrates a clear correlation between depression and negative thinking. (AO3=3)

However, faulty cognitions may be a symptom or consequence of depression rather than the cause. The person may have a biological abnormality that causes negative thinking. This theory also is reductionist as it reduces complex human phenomena into simplistic human terminology and it does not take into account both behavioural and biological influences. (AO3=3)

(184   words)

Section C
Research Methods

Answer __all__ questions in this section (30 minutes for each section on Paper 2)

Read the item and then answer the questions that follow.

Two researchers obtained a sample of ten people whose ages ranged from 20-years-old to 60-years-old.

Each participant was asked to take part in a discussion of social care issues. This included discussion about who should pay for social care for elderly people and how to deal with people struggling with mental health problems. A confederate of the researchers was given a script to follow in which a series of discussion points was written for the confederate to introduce.

Each participant then came into a room individually and the discussion with the confederate took place. The maximum time allowed for a discussion was 30 minutes.

The researchers observed the discussions between the confederate and participants and rated the active engagement of the participants in the discussion. The ratings were between 1, (not at all interested) and 20, (extremely interested.) The researchers believed that the rating provided a measurement of the participants' attitudes towards social care issues.

The following data were obtained in the study:

Table 2: The relationship between age and attitude to social care

Age of participant	Attitude to social care issues rating
21	5
23	3

34	8
36	12
40	10
47	13
52	17
53	15
58	18
60	20

0 1 What does the table suggest about the relationship between age and attitude to social care issues? Explain your answer.

[2 marks] (2.5 minutes) (AO2 = 2) (50 words maximum)

The table suggests a positive correlation between the age of the participant and their attitude to social care issues. The relationship between age and attitude to social care issues shows that as the age of the participant increases so does their attitude to social care issues rating generally.

(48 words)

0 2 The researchers rated the active engagement of the participants in the discussion on social care. They used this rating as a measure of each participant's attitude to social care issues. Briefly explain how investigator effects might have occurred in this study.

[2 marks] (2.5 minutes) (AO2 = 2) (50 words maximum)

The investigator effect is when the investigator has knowledge of the research aim and this knowledge affects the data collected. This can affect results as the experimenter may have preconceived ideas as to how age affects our levels of interest in social care issues.

(44 words)

0 3 Outline how the researchers could have avoided investigator effects having an impact on the study.

[2 marks] (2.5 minutes) (AO3 = 2) (50 words maximum)

Investigator effects could have been nullified by having two researchers assess the group discussion and comparing their scores to see if they match or are similar. This is known as inter-rater/observer reliability.

(32 words)

0 4 The researchers thought it might be interesting to investigate further the attitudes of the participants in the study. They decided to interview each participant. The researchers devised a questionnaire in order to collect the data they required. The questionnaire included both open and closed questions.

Briefly discuss the benefits for the researchers of using both closed and open questions on their questionnaire about attitudes to social care.

[4 marks] (5 minutes) (AO2 = 4) (100 words maximum)

Closed questions enable researchers to obtain quantitative data (facts, figures, known as hard data etc.) which is easy to analyse and draw conclusions from. However closed questions only collect data that the researchers believe to be relevant. It is therefore useful to use open questions also as they collect qualitative data (thoughts, feelings, known as soft data etc.) and this enables the researchers to have the participants expand upon their answers. Therefore, there are clear advantages to using both closed and open questions in a questionnaire about attitudes to social care for a researcher.

(94 words)

0 5 Write one question that you think the researchers might have put on their questionnaire. Explain which type of question you have written and why you think this would be a suitable question for this study.

[3 marks] (3.75 minutes) (AO2 = 3) (75 words maximum)

'Have you researched the types of social care that are available in this country?' This is a closed question and thus enables the researcher to collect quantitative data which is easier to analyse than qualitative data.

(36 words)

0 6 The researchers have obtained both qualitative and quantitative data in the observations and interviews they have conducted.

Identify the qualitative and quantitative data collected in this study. Explain your answer.

[4 marks] (5 minutes) (AO1 = 2; AO2 = 2) (100 words maximum)

Quantitative data is collected from closed questions and will be numerically based, facts, figures etc. and is sometimes known as hard data i.e. a score represented in the form of a score on a scale.

Qualitative data is collected from open questions and is descriptive of thoughts, feelings and emotions etc. and could be found in the attitude' ratings.

(59 words)

0 7 Explain how the researchers should have addressed two ethical issues in the investigation.

[4 marks] (5 minutes) (AO3 = 4) (100 words maximum)

The right to withdraw is an ethical issue that should have been made clear to the participants in order to ensure that they are clearly aware that they can withdraw from the experiment at any time without facing negative consequences.

A second ethical issue that should have been addressed is informed consent. This should be obtained and the participants should be forewarned of what the experiment will entail and be briefed and debriefed and they should also be given clear information as to what the investigation will involve.

(88   words)

HOW TO SUCCEED IN AN INTERVIEW!

You may have an interview in order to secure an offer from your University of choice; therefore, I have included this article I wrote as regards succeeding in an interview. The information here applies to academic or job interviews and it will give you both the best chance of succeeding and significantly reduce any tension you feel as regards interviews if you follow the simple principles outlined below.

"When we have tasks, we can feel overwhelmed and I use the metaphor of cutting down a tree to describe this. At first, the whole tree seems overwhelming but as you begin to cut it down you feel differently. *You do not begin to feel differently when the tree is cut down but as soon as you start to cut it.* Therefore, just do the next right thing, work within compartments of an hour by hour basis. It is the anticipation of an event that gives us fear that is worse than the event itself. *Perhaps during but definitely after your interview, I promise you, you will feel better.*

Preparation is important and being calm and going to the interview feeling relaxed (as much as is possible) is important. Have the clothes on that you feel good in and get to the interview with plenty of time to spare; this is really important! Also aim to sleep as well as you can the night before the interview but accept it calmly if you are unable to.

Everyone is in the same boat as you. All the other people who are being interviewed are nervous too. The interviewers want to see someone good! You are good! Sometimes, in these situations I have feared secretly that I wasn't good enough. <u>However, the interviewers are good and you are good</u>! There is nothing to hide, you can enjoy this, honest! It is a chance to show people what you would like to do if you worked/studied with them. If they asked you for an interview, they already like you. At the end of the interview, if you still want the place/position say, "I want to re-state my interest in working here/being a student at this University. Thank you". However only say this if you mean it. Remember you are interviewing them too; they want a good employee and/or student also. Remember there is nothing more similar to us, which we can relate to more, than another human being. They are all human!

If you have a panel interview this may perhaps be the hardest part of the day; but not necessarily! I have had a panel interview before and I was a little nervous but everyone else who was interviewed would have been nervous too and the panel are expecting that. *However, as long as you are yourself and comfortable, then if the job or place is meant to be yours, it will be. If not, it won't.* Sometimes courses and jobs don't suit us and it is as important to know what we don't want as to know what we do. If you just do your best, you can't do any more than that. You may feel nervous, that is ok! Please don't beat yourself up for beating yourself up; mental double-edged clubs are no good. If you feel bad or nervous before or during the interview, that is ok; accept it (then it usually lessens). Just think about how good you will feel after the interview is done. Just be yourself, that is always enough, *no matter what you are doing in your life* and if we make mistakes, they are great, as they teach us something about the next time we are in the same situation."

I wish you every success in all your interviews to come and I hope and know that the advice above can help.

Very best wishes and thank you for purchasing this book,

Joseph

Printed in Great Britain
by Amazon